Christopher, please clean up your room!

Itah Sadu

Illustrations by
Roy Condy

McGraw Hill SRA

Columbus, OH

To my nieces Michelle Blackman and Luleka Keyi—
shining stars.
Itah

Published by arrangement with Scholastic, Canada Ltd.

SRAonline.com

SRA

Printed in the U.S.A.

Send all inquiries to:
SRA/McGraw-Hill
4400 Easton Commons
Columbus, OH 43219-6188

ISBN 978-0-07-612494-7
MHID 0-07-612494-0

11 12 13 BRP 24

The McGraw·Hill Companies

Christopher lived on Glenplace Avenue with his family. He was a fine young man, who helped his neighbors with errands and did his chores. He was good at sports and came first in his class.

The one thing Christopher *wouldn't* do was clean his room.

His clothes were scattered around. Books, papers and magazines lay all over the floor. The dust was piling up. Christopher's room *stank!*

The socks under the bed were cheesy
the sandwich behind the door grew fungi
the room was so untidy
the shoes smelled funky funky
and the fish bowl stank!

Christopher's mother refused to go into his room because she thought there might be snakes in there. His grandmother, when she visited, always fainted. His father never went too near Christopher's door, and when his friends slept over they had nightmares about rats. Even the wind wouldn't blow through Christophers room.

When his family and his friends complained, Christopher just said, "I like my room the way it is. I can find everything. It's comfortable like this."

And he refused to clean his room.

His parents tried everything. Christopher couldn't have dessert, but he wouldn't clean his room. He couldn't watch TV, but he wouldn't clean his room. He wasn't allowed to have friends over, but he wouldn't clean his room.

The socks under the bed were cheesy
the sandwich behind the door grew fungi
the room was so untidy
the shoes smelled funky funky
and the fish bowl stank!

Now, the two goldfish who lived in that fish bowl were becoming quite concerned about their health. Christopher had not changed the water in their bowl in weeks, and it was green and murky. They felt like they were choking.

So the goldfish decided to find a way to get Christopher to clean his room. All that day they thought and talked, but they couldn't come up with a plan. That night, as they were having supper, they spotted a cockroach hurrying across the room.

"Mr. Cockroach, wait up. Mr. Cockroach, a word with you," one fish said.

The cockroach stopped and climbed up to the fish bowl. "Good evening, Ms. Fish, Ms. Fish. What can I do for you?" he asked.

"We need you to help us do a job," replied the fish. "We need to get Christopher to clean up his room."

"Oh, no indeed," said Mr. Cockroach. "I can't stay here. This room is much too dirty, much too dirty. I only take shortcuts through here to get next door. And besides, he likes it like this. He'll never clean up."

"What about your friends? Would they help?" asked the fish. "They feel the same way," replied Mr. Cockroach. "They can't stand to come in here.

"The socks under the bed are cheesy
the sandwich behind the door grows fungi
the room is so untidy
the shoes smell funky funky
and the fish bowl stinks!"

The fish started to cry. No one would help them. They were doomed.

Mr. Cockroach looked at the floor. He hated to see fish cry. He felt sorry for them, but what could he do?

Suddenly he had an idea.

"Don't cry," he said. "I will speak to my people, and let you know what we can do." And he went off to the big sugar feast at the store next door.

That night the cockroaches met and planned. Word was sent to the goldfish. The fish were happy, because they knew that the cockroaches were just right for the job.

At 11:30 it began. Thousands of cockroaches had gathered: cockroaches from the east and from the west, cockroaches from the north and the south. There were cockroaches of every kind.

They put on their gas masks, and at 11:45 they started to crawl toward Christopher's room.

Christopher was sound asleep. He had played a good game of baseball that day, shared a sundae with his friend Hal, and had once more refused to clean his room. Someday when he was older he might clean it up but for now it was comfortable the way it was.

The socks under the bed were cheesy
the sandwich behind the door grew fungi
the room was so untidy
the shoes smelled funky funky
and the fish bowl stank!

By 11:55 the cockroaches were in place. The goldfish looked on as roaches landed all over the room. Every surface was covered in a mixture of shades and colors.

At midnight it began. A cockroach dropped on Christopher's eye and he blinked. Another one dropped on his nose and he brushed it away. Suddenly one dropped in his mouth and he woke up with a start.

He turned on the lights, but he could not scream. He was too shocked. He tried to brush the cockroaches off his bed, but they kept coming and coming. Then the ones on the wall started to move.

They spelled out:

CHRISTOPHER, TIDY UP YOUR ROOM NOW!

"I'll do it tomorrow," Christopher said.

The cockroaches replied:

TIDY UP YOUR ROOM NOW.

WE MEAN BUSINESS.

And they started coming toward him: blue roaches, grey roaches, black roaches, brown roaches, striped ones and polka-dotted ones—all kinds of cockroaches.

They surrounded his bed—fat ones, skinny ones, big ones, small ones. And they kept coming.

Christopher was terrified. He jumped out of bed and ran for the closet, where he got the duster, the broom, the vacuum, and a laundry basket. Quickly he started to pack up all his clothes and put them away.

He looked up, and a quarter of the cockroaches were gone.

He dusted his books and shelves, tidied his papers, and looked again. Another quarter of the cockroaches were gone. He swept and vacuumed and another quarter of the cockroaches went away.

He cleaned all under his bed and the last quarter of the roaches went away, except for Mr. Cockroach who stood on the dresser by the fish bowl.

Christopher opened his window, and he took the fish bowl for a good cleaning. When he returned, Mr. Cockroach went away too.

The fish were happy and the wind blew through the room again. Everything was nice and clean, light and bright, spic and span. Even Christopher felt better. He jumped back into his bed and fell fast asleep.

The next morning Christopher's family was amazed. His mother came to see his room, his father came to see his room, his grandmother came to see his room, even his friends came to see his room.

But they were puzzled. What had come over Christopher?

Well, Christopher isn't talking, but any time there is a speck or a spot, a pile of dust, a crumb on the floor or a bunch of clothes on the chair, Christopher cleans up.

He remembers only too well the night of the cockroaches.